# Data-Driven Deals

*Leveraging Technology for Real Estate Success*

**NELLA BYRAN**

**Copyright**

**No part of this should be reproduced without the permission of the author.**

© Nella Byran 2024

# Contents

Introduction ................................................................. 4
The Power of Data ....................................................... 8
Data Mining and Market Analysis ................................ 13
Predictive Analytics .................................................... 18
Staying Agile in a Dynamic Market .............................. 23
Artificial Intelligence in Real Estate ............................. 29
Machine Learning Models ........................................... 35
Data Visualization: Communicating Insights for Clarity .. 40
Location Intelligence .................................................. 45
Customer Segmentation: Tailoring Deals for Maximum Impact ........................................................................ 52
Transactional Data Management ................................ 59
Competitive Analysis .................................................. 66
Marketing Strategies for Data-Driven Deals ................ 72
Risk Assessment Models: Minimizing Losses with Data .. 81
Data Privacy and Security in Real Estate ..................... 88
Ethical Use of Data: Ensuring Fairness and Transparency 95
Regulatory Compliance in a Data-Driven World ......... 103
The Future of Data in Real Estate .............................. 112
Conclusion ............................................................... 120

# Introduction

Welcome to "Data-Driven Deals: Leveraging Technology for Real Estate Success," a comprehensive guide that illuminates the transformative impact of data analytics, artificial intelligence, and cutting-edge technologies on the world of property transactions.

In the fast-evolving landscape of real estate, success is no longer solely reliant on instinct or traditional market wisdom. Instead, it hinges on the ability to harness the power of data. This book serves as a roadmap for investors, developers, and agents, guiding them through the intricate realm where data is the cornerstone of strategic decision-making.

The journey begins with understanding the fundamental shift brought about by data. We explore how data illuminates trends, identifies opportunities, and empowers stakeholders to make informed choices that drive profitability and mitigate risks. From data mining and market analysis to predictive analytics and real-time data streams, each chapter unveils a vital aspect of leveraging data for real estate success.

Artificial intelligence (AI) and machine learning are no longer distant concepts but integral tools enhancing deal efficiency and automating processes. Readers will discover how AI-powered tools streamline property valuations, customer interactions, and marketing strategies, creating a more seamless experience for all involved.

Location intelligence, customer segmentation, and competitive analysis are explored to showcase how data refines strategies. By tailoring deals to specific buyer segments and benchmarking against competitors, stakeholders gain a strategic edge in the market.

Efficiency is paramount in real estate transactions, and readers will learn how data-driven transactional data management optimizes deal cycles, reduces bottlenecks, and ensures smoother processes from listing to closing.

With great data power comes great responsibility. Ethical considerations in data usage are addressed, from fair housing practices to transparency in decision-making. Compliance with regulatory frameworks is crucial in this data-driven world, and readers will gain insights into navigating GDPR and other legal requirements.

As we conclude our journey, a glimpse into the future of real estate is provided. Augmented reality property tours, blockchain-based transactions, and other innovations are on the horizon. By staying informed and adaptable, stakeholders can position themselves for success in the ever-evolving world of data-driven real estate.

Whether you're a seasoned investor, a developer scouting new opportunities, or an agent seeking to provide unparalleled service to clients, "Data-

Driven Deals" equips you with the knowledge and tools to thrive in this new era. So, let's dive in and discover the future of real estate—one data point at a time.

## *The Power of Data*

In the realm of real estate, where fortunes are made and lost with each transaction, the power of data has emerged as a formidable force, reshaping the very foundations of decision-making. Imagine a world where every move, every investment, and every strategy is guided not by hunches or historical anecdotes, but by a deep understanding of current trends, market dynamics, and predictive insights. This is the world that the power of data has brought to real estate professionals.

At its core, the power of data is about transforming uncertainty into clarity. Gone are the days of relying solely on gut feelings or traditional market wisdom. Today, data serves as the guiding light, illuminating the path to profitable investments and mitigating risks that once loomed large. Consider the investor who, armed with comprehensive market data and analysis, can confidently identify emerging neighborhoods poised for growth. What was once a leap of faith is now a calculated decision, backed by robust data points and predictive models.

Data empowers real estate professionals to see beyond the surface, uncovering hidden opportunities that may have remained invisible in the past. Through sophisticated data mining techniques, vast troves of information are sifted through to reveal patterns, trends, and anomalies. Picture a developer poring over demographic data, understanding not just the current population trends but also the projected growth patterns over the next decade. Armed with this insight, they can make strategic decisions about where to build the next residential community or commercial hub.

One of the most captivating aspects of the power of data is its ability to forecast the future with uncanny accuracy. Predictive analytics, fueled by historical data and advanced algorithms, enables stakeholders to peer into the crystal ball of real estate. It's not about mere speculation; it's about forecasting property appreciation rates, foreseeing shifts in demand, and identifying upcoming market trends. This foresight transforms the guessing game of real estate into a science, where decisions are made with a confidence born of data-driven insights.

Real estate is inherently dynamic, with market conditions shifting rapidly. Here, real-time data streams become invaluable. Imagine an agent receiving instant updates on new listings, price changes, or competitor activities. This real-time awareness allows for agile decision-making, seizing opportunities the moment they arise and adapting strategies in response to changing market dynamics. The ability to stay ahead of the curve in a fast-moving market is a game-changer, and real-time data provides the competitive edge needed to thrive.

The power of data isn't just about numbers and statistics; it's about leveraging artificial intelligence (AI) to revolutionize real estate decision-making. AI-powered tools are transforming everything from property valuations to customer interactions. Picture an AI system analyzing vast datasets to generate accurate property valuations in minutes, taking into account a myriad of factors that would take human appraisers days to process. This efficiency not only saves time but also enhances accuracy, ensuring that deals are based on precise and up-to-date information.

In essence, the power of data in real estate is about transforming information into actionable intelligence. It's about arming professionals with the tools and insights they need to make confident, informed decisions. Whether it's uncovering hidden opportunities through data mining, forecasting future trends with predictive analytics, staying agile with real-time data streams, or harnessing AI for efficiency, data has become the cornerstone of success in the modern real estate landscape.

For those willing to embrace this new era of data-driven decision-making, the rewards are substantial. It's no longer a question of "what if" but rather "what's next." The power of data has ushered in a new era of precision and clarity in real estate, where informed choices pave the way to profitability and success. As we delve deeper into the chapters ahead, we will continue to explore how data is not just a tool but a transformative force that is reshaping the very essence of real estate decision-making. So, buckle up and prepare to embark on a journey where the power of data unlocks the doors to new possibilities in the world of real estate.

# Data Mining and Market Analysis

In the intricate tapestry of real estate, where every decision can have significant financial implications, the art of data mining and market analysis emerges as a potent tool for uncovering hidden opportunities. Imagine peering beneath the surface of a seemingly static market, where properties rise and fall, neighborhoods evolve, and buyer preferences shift. This is where data mining shines, revealing patterns and trends that can guide investors, developers, and agents toward lucrative opportunities.

Data mining, at its core, is the process of extracting meaningful patterns and insights from vast datasets. In the context of real estate, this means delving into a wealth of information ranging from property prices and historical sales data to demographic trends and economic indicators. Imagine a real estate professional utilizing data mining techniques to uncover neighborhoods with a high potential for growth. By analyzing historical sales data, population trends, and economic indicators, they can identify areas where property values are likely to appreciate in the coming years.

One of the key advantages of data mining in real estate is its ability to identify emerging trends before they become widely recognized. Consider a developer looking to build a new residential complex. By analyzing data on population growth, employment trends, and infrastructure development, they can pinpoint areas where demand for housing is likely to surge. This foresight allows them to secure land or properties at favorable prices before the market catches on, maximizing their return on investment.

Market analysis, closely intertwined with data mining, takes these insights to the next level. It's not just about uncovering trends; it's about understanding the market dynamics that drive them. Picture a market analyst examining a local housing market, dissecting factors such as supply and demand, median income levels, and housing affordability. By synthesizing these variables, they can paint a comprehensive picture of the market's health and identify niches ripe for exploration.

In the realm of real estate investment, data mining and market analysis are invaluable for identifying undervalued properties. Imagine an investor combing through property listings, analyzing historical sales data, neighborhood crime rates, school ratings, and proximity to amenities. By applying data-driven analytics, they can pinpoint properties that are priced below market value, presenting an opportunity for substantial returns upon renovation or resale.

Moreover, data mining and market analysis empower real estate professionals to tailor their strategies to specific market segments. Consider an agent specializing in luxury properties. By analyzing demographic data and buyer preferences, they can craft targeted marketing campaigns that resonate with high-net-worth individuals. This personalized approach increases the likelihood of attracting qualified buyers and closing deals swiftly.

For developers, data mining and market analysis are essential for determining the viability of new projects. Before breaking ground on a new residential community or commercial complex, they delve into data on zoning regulations, construction costs, and market demand. This thorough analysis minimizes the risk of investing in projects that may not align with market needs or face regulatory hurdles.

The beauty of data mining and market analysis in real estate lies in their ability to transform ambiguity into opportunity. What was once a landscape shrouded in uncertainty becomes a canvas for strategic decision-making. Whether it's identifying emerging neighborhoods, uncovering undervalued properties, or tailoring strategies to specific market segments, data-driven insights pave the way for success.

As we delve deeper into the world of data-driven real estate, we will continue to explore how data mining and market analysis are not just tools but gateways to uncovering opportunities that may have otherwise remained hidden. So, buckle up and prepare to embark on a journey where the power of data illuminates the path to profitable investments and strategic decisions in the dynamic world of real estate.

## *Predictive Analytics*

In the dynamic world of real estate, where fortunes rise and fall with market shifts, predictive analytics emerges as a powerful tool for those seeking to stay ahead of the curve. Imagine a world where investors, developers, and agents can foresee market trends with a clarity that borders on prescience. This is the realm of predictive analytics, where historical data and advanced algorithms converge to illuminate the path to profitable deals.

At its core, predictive analytics is about more than just educated guesses; it's about harnessing the power of data to forecast future trends with remarkable accuracy. Picture an investor contemplating a property purchase. Instead of relying solely on current market conditions or gut feelings, they turn to predictive analytics to assess the property's potential for appreciation. By analyzing historical sales data, neighborhood growth patterns, and economic indicators, they can generate a data-driven projection of future property values.

One of the key benefits of predictive analytics in real estate is its ability to identify emerging trends before they become widely recognized. Consider a developer considering the next location for a residential project. By analyzing demographic shifts, employment trends, and infrastructure developments, they can pinpoint areas poised for growth. Armed with this insight, they can secure properties at favorable prices before demand surges, maximizing their return on investment.

For agents working with buyers, predictive analytics offers a strategic advantage in matching clients with properties that align with their future needs. Imagine an agent utilizing predictive models to anticipate neighborhood trends and lifestyle preferences. By understanding a buyer's long-term goals, such as proximity to schools or upcoming developments, they can recommend properties that not only meet current needs but also align with future aspirations.

In the realm of property management, predictive analytics can revolutionize decision-making. Property managers can use predictive models to anticipate maintenance needs, tenant turnover rates, and optimal rental pricing. By forecasting these variables, they can proactively address issues before they escalate, maximize occupancy rates, and optimize rental income.

Moreover, predictive analytics can play a pivotal role in risk management. Real estate investments inherently carry risks, from market fluctuations to unforeseen events. Predictive models can assess the likelihood of risks such as vacancy rates, interest rate changes, or economic downturns. Armed with this knowledge, investors can implement risk mitigation strategies, such as diversifying their portfolios or adjusting financing terms.

One of the most captivating aspects of predictive analytics is its ability to adapt and learn from new data. As market conditions evolve, predictive models can incorporate real-time data streams to refine their forecasts. This agility ensures that decisions remain informed and relevant in an ever-changing landscape.

For stakeholders across the real estate spectrum, from investors to agents to developers, predictive analytics offers a glimpse into the future, guiding decisions with a level of foresight that was once unimaginable. It transforms uncertainty into opportunity, allowing professionals to navigate the complexities of the market with confidence.

As we journey through the realm of data-driven real estate, we will continue to explore the transformative potential of predictive analytics. From forecasting property appreciation rates to anticipating market shifts, this tool empowers stakeholders to make strategic decisions that pave the way for profitable deals. So, let us embrace the power of predictive analytics as we navigate the dynamic landscape of real estate, where the future is not just a guess but a data-driven projection toward success.

# Staying Agile in a Dynamic Market

In the fast-paced and ever-evolving world of real estate, staying agile is not just a competitive advantage—it's a necessity. This is where real-time data streams become a game-changer, providing professionals with up-to-the-minute insights that enable swift and informed decision-making. Imagine a market where opportunities arise and disappear in the blink of an eye, where being a step ahead can make all the difference. Real-time data streams are the pulse of this market, offering a constant flow of information that allows stakeholders to adapt and thrive.

At its core, real-time data streams are a continuous feed of information from a variety of sources, including listing platforms, market reports, social media, and more. These streams provide a live, unfiltered view of the market landscape, allowing professionals to monitor trends, competitor activities, and new listings as they happen. Picture an agent receiving instant alerts on price reductions in a sought-after neighborhood or a developer tracking changes in zoning regulations that could impact a planned project. This immediacy empowers stakeholders to act decisively and seize opportunities before they slip away.

One of the primary benefits of real-time data streams is their ability to enhance market intelligence. Imagine an investor analyzing a specific neighborhood for potential investment. By tapping into real-time data streams, they can monitor factors such as median home prices, days on market, and inventory levels in real-time. This granular level of insight allows them to gauge the competitiveness of the market and make informed decisions about pricing strategies or timing for entering or exiting the market.

For agents working with buyers, real-time data streams offer a competitive edge in finding the perfect property. Imagine a buyer with specific criteria, such as a preference for homes with a backyard and proximity to schools. With real-time data streams, an agent can set up automated alerts that notify them the moment a property meeting these criteria hits the market. This proactive approach ensures that clients are among the first to know about new listings that align with their needs, increasing their chances of securing their dream home.

In the realm of property management, real-time data streams revolutionize maintenance and tenant relations. Property managers can utilize IoT (Internet of Things) devices to monitor building systems, such as HVAC or plumbing, in real-time. If a sensor detects an issue, such as a water leak or malfunctioning equipment, alerts are sent immediately, allowing for swift action to prevent damage and costly repairs. Additionally, real-time data on tenant behavior and preferences can be used to enhance tenant satisfaction, such as offering personalized services or amenities.

Real-time data streams are also invaluable for developers navigating the complexities of project planning and execution. Imagine a developer overseeing a large-scale construction project. By integrating real-time data on construction progress, supply chain logistics, and weather conditions, they can optimize scheduling and resource allocation on the fly. This agility minimizes delays and cost overruns, ensuring projects stay on track and within budget.

Moreover, real-time data streams enable professionals to monitor competitor activities and market trends with unprecedented granularity. Picture a brokerage analyzing pricing trends in a specific neighborhood compared to competitors. By accessing real-time data on recent sales and listing prices, they can adjust their pricing strategies to remain competitive and attract more clients.

In an age where information is power, real-time data streams empower real estate professionals to be proactive rather than reactive. This agility is particularly crucial in a dynamic market where conditions can change rapidly. Whether it's seizing opportunities, optimizing pricing strategies, enhancing client service, or streamlining operations, real-time data streams are the linchpin that keeps professionals ahead of the curve.

As we navigate the world of data-driven real estate, the role of real-time data streams becomes increasingly central. From agents to investors to developers, the ability to access and leverage real-time insights is a game-changer. It's not just about reacting to market shifts; it's about anticipating them and staying one step ahead. So, let us embrace the power of real-time data streams as we navigate the dynamic and ever-evolving landscape of real estate, where agility and informed decision-making pave the way for success.

# Artificial Intelligence in Real Estate

In the digital age, the integration of artificial intelligence (AI) into the real estate sector represents a seismic shift in how deals are executed, analyzed, and optimized. Imagine a world where tasks that once required hours of manual effort are completed in minutes with unparalleled accuracy. This is the promise of AI in real estate, where efficiency is not just a goal but a reality reshaping the industry.

At its core, AI in real estate is about using advanced algorithms and machine learning to automate and optimize processes that traditionally relied on human judgment. Picture an AI system analyzing vast datasets, from property listings and historical sales data to market trends and customer preferences. This analysis allows for more precise property valuations, pricing strategies, and targeted marketing efforts.

One of the most significant contributions of AI to real estate is in property valuations. Traditionally, valuing a property required extensive research, comparable sales analysis, and manual calculations. With AI-powered valuation tools, this process is revolutionized. Imagine an AI system analyzing thousands of data points, such as property size, location, amenities, and market trends, to generate an accurate valuation within minutes. This not only saves time but also reduces the margin of error, ensuring that deals are based on precise and up-to-date information.

For agents, AI acts as a virtual assistant, streamlining tasks and enhancing customer service. Imagine an agent with an AI chatbot that can instantly respond to client inquiries, schedule appointments, and provide property recommendations based on personalized preferences. This level of responsiveness and efficiency not only improves the client experience but also frees up the agent's time to focus on building relationships and closing deals.

AI also plays a pivotal role in customer segmentation and targeted marketing. Real estate professionals can leverage AI to analyze customer data and behavior, segmenting clients into specific categories based on preferences, buying patterns, and demographics. This segmentation allows for highly targeted marketing campaigns that resonate with specific audiences, increasing the likelihood of attracting qualified leads and closing deals.

Moreover, AI is transforming the way properties are marketed and showcased to potential buyers. Virtual reality (VR) and augmented reality (AR) technologies, powered by AI algorithms, allow for immersive property tours from the comfort of a computer or smartphone. Imagine a buyer walking through a virtual representation of a property, exploring every room and detail as if they were physically present. This technology not only enhances the buyer experience but also expands the reach of properties to global audiences.

In the realm of property management, AI-driven predictive maintenance is a game-changer. Property managers can utilize AI to analyze data from IoT devices, such as sensors monitoring building systems, to predict maintenance needs before they escalate. By detecting potential issues, such as HVAC malfunctions or water leaks, in advance, property managers can proactively address them, reducing downtime and costly repairs.

AI also optimizes deal cycles and transaction processes. From automating document processing and compliance checks to identifying potential risks and fraud, AI streamlines the entire deal lifecycle. Imagine a seamless transaction where contracts are reviewed, verified, and executed with

AI-powered tools that ensure accuracy and compliance with legal requirements. This efficiency not only reduces administrative burdens but also minimizes errors and delays in closing deals.

The potential of AI in real estate is vast and transformative. As we continue to explore its applications, from property valuations to customer service and marketing, one thing becomes clear: AI is not just a tool; it's a catalyst for efficiency and innovation. By embracing AI, real estate professionals can unlock new levels of productivity, precision, and profitability in an industry that thrives on speed and accuracy.

As we journey through the realm of AI-driven real estate, we will continue to witness its impact on enhancing deal efficiency. From automating tasks to optimizing processes, AI is reshaping the landscape of real estate transactions. So, let us embrace the power of AI as we navigate the evolving and dynamic world of real estate, where efficiency is not just a goal but a reality that drives success.

# Machine Learning Models

In the realm of real estate, property valuation is a critical and often time-consuming process that requires careful analysis of various factors. Enter machine learning, a revolutionary technology that is transforming the way property valuations are conducted. Imagine a world where the valuation of a property is not reliant on manual calculations and historical data alone, but on sophisticated algorithms that can analyze vast amounts of information with speed and precision. This is the promise of machine learning in real estate, where automation enhances efficiency and accuracy in property valuations.

At its core, machine learning involves the development of algorithms that can learn from data and make predictions or decisions based on that data. In the context of real estate, machine learning models are trained on diverse datasets, including property attributes, historical sales data, market trends, and more. These models then use this data to generate property valuations that are tailored to specific factors affecting the market.

One of the primary benefits of machine learning in property valuations is its ability to handle complex and multifaceted data. Imagine a property with numerous attributes such as size, location, number of bedrooms, amenities, and more. Traditionally, valuing such a property would require manual analysis and comparison with similar properties. With machine learning, these attributes can be fed into the model, which then considers how each factor contributes to the property's overall value. This level of granularity allows for more accurate and nuanced valuations.

Moreover, machine learning models excel at identifying patterns and trends within datasets that may not be immediately apparent to human appraisers. For example, a machine learning model can analyze historical sales data to detect subtle shifts in property values based on factors such as neighborhood development, school district changes, or economic indicators. This insight enables the model to adapt and adjust valuations in real-time, reflecting the dynamic nature of the market.

One of the most captivating aspects of machine learning in property valuations is its ability to learn and improve over time. As the model is exposed to more data and outcomes, it continuously refines its algorithms, becoming more accurate and reliable. This means that with each valuation, the model becomes better at predicting property values with precision, incorporating new market trends and factors as they emerge.

For real estate professionals, machine learning models offer a transformative approach to property valuations. Picture an agent or investor using a machine learning-powered valuation tool to assess multiple properties in minutes, instead of hours or days. This efficiency not only saves time but also allows for more comprehensive analysis of a broader range of properties. Additionally, machine learning models provide transparency in the valuation process, as they can explain how they arrived at a particular valuation, giving stakeholders confidence in the results.

In the realm of real estate investment, machine learning models are invaluable for portfolio optimization. Investors can utilize these models to analyze large portfolios of properties, identifying those that are undervalued or have the potential for appreciation. By incorporating data on rental income, vacancy rates, and market trends, the model can provide recommendations on which properties to acquire, hold, or sell, maximizing returns.

Furthermore, machine learning models enhance risk assessment in real estate transactions. Whether it's assessing the risk of default on a mortgage or evaluating the potential for property depreciation, these models can analyze a wide range of variables to quantify and mitigate risks. This proactive approach to risk management allows investors and lenders to make informed decisions and minimize potential losses.

As we journey through the realm of machine learning in real estate, the impact on property valuations is profound. From automating tasks to providing accurate and transparent valuations, machine learning models are revolutionizing the industry. So, let us embrace the power of machine learning as we navigate the evolving and dynamic world of real estate, where automation and precision drive efficiency and success.

# Data Visualization: Communicating Insights for Clarity

In the vast landscape of real estate data, the ability to extract meaningful insights and communicate them effectively is paramount. This is where data visualization steps in as a powerful tool, transforming complex datasets into clear, compelling visuals that provide clarity and understanding. Imagine a world where trends, patterns, and correlations are not buried in spreadsheets and reports but are brought to life through interactive charts, graphs, and maps. This is the promise of data visualization in real estate, where insights become accessible and actionable for stakeholders.

At its core, data visualization is about more than just creating pretty pictures—it's about distilling complex information into visual representations that are easy to comprehend and interpret. In the context of real estate, this means turning vast amounts of data, such as property sales, market trends, demographic information, and geographic data, into visualizations that tell a story.

One of the primary benefits of data visualization in real estate is its ability to uncover hidden patterns and trends that may not be immediately apparent in raw data. Imagine a real estate agent analyzing property sales over time in a specific neighborhood. By plotting this data on a time series graph, trends such as seasonal fluctuations or long-term appreciation become clear at a glance. This insight allows agents to advise clients on the best time to buy or sell, based on historical trends.

Moreover, data visualization enables stakeholders to compare and contrast data points effortlessly. For example, imagine an investor considering multiple properties for acquisition. With a side-by-side comparison chart, they can easily assess key metrics such as price per square foot, rental income potential, and vacancy rates. This visual comparison streamlines the decision-making process and allows for a more comprehensive analysis of investment opportunities.

Interactive maps are another powerful tool in the data visualization toolkit. Picture a developer exploring potential locations for a new residential development. By overlaying demographic data, school ratings, and transportation networks on a map, they can identify areas that align with their target market. Interactive maps allow for zooming in on specific areas, clicking on data points for more information, and filtering by criteria such as income levels or age demographics. This interactive exploration not only provides a holistic view of the market but also allows for a deeper understanding of the factors influencing property values.

In the realm of market analysis, data visualization is indispensable for identifying market trends and making informed predictions. Imagine an analyst creating a heat map of property prices across a city, with colors indicating high and low values. This visualization immediately highlights areas of opportunity or areas where prices may be overheated. Additionally, trend lines and regression plots can visually represent market trends, allowing stakeholders to anticipate future movements and adjust strategies accordingly.

For real estate professionals, data visualization is not just a tool for analysis—it's a powerful communication tool. Imagine a comprehensive market report presented to clients, filled with interactive charts and infographics that illustrate market trends, demographic profiles, and investment opportunities. This visual storytelling not only engages clients but also helps them understand complex concepts with ease.

In the realm of property marketing, data visualization plays a crucial role in showcasing properties to potential buyers. Virtual tours, 3D floor plans, and interactive property maps bring listings to life, allowing buyers to explore properties in detail from anywhere in the world. High-resolution images, videos, and virtual reality experiences immerse buyers in the property, helping them envision themselves living or working there.

As we navigate the world of data-driven real estate, the role of data visualization becomes increasingly central. From agents to investors to developers, the ability to access and leverage visual insights is a game-changer. It's not just about analyzing data; it's about telling a compelling story that informs decisions and drives action. So, let us embrace the power of data visualization as we navigate the evolving and dynamic world of real estate, where clarity and understanding pave the way for success.

## *Location Intelligence*

In the world of real estate, the age-old adage "location, location, location" continues to ring true. However, in the era of data-driven decision-making, this mantra has evolved into a sophisticated concept known as location intelligence. Imagine a world where the success of a property investment hinges not just on its physical attributes, but on a comprehensive understanding of its surrounding environment—demographics, amenities, infrastructure, market trends, and more. This is the realm of location intelligence, where strategic property investments are guided by a deep analysis of location-based data.

At its core, location intelligence is about harnessing the power of spatial data and analytics to gain valuable insights into the geographic context of a property. In the context of real estate investments, location intelligence serves as a compass, guiding investors, developers, and agents toward properties with the highest potential for appreciation and returns.

One of the primary aspects of location intelligence is demographic analysis. Imagine an investor considering a residential property in a particular neighborhood. By analyzing demographic data, such as age distribution, income levels, household size, and education levels, they can gain insights into the type of residents who live in the area. This information is invaluable for determining the target market for the property—whether it's young professionals seeking urban amenities, families looking for good schools, or retirees seeking a quiet lifestyle.

Moreover, location intelligence allows investors to assess the economic health of an area. Imagine analyzing employment data, job growth rates, and industry diversification to understand the economic stability and potential for growth in a location. A thriving job market and diverse industries indicate a robust local economy, which can drive demand for housing and lead to property appreciation. Conversely, areas with declining job opportunities may signal potential risks for investment.

Infrastructure and amenities play a crucial role in location intelligence. Imagine a developer evaluating a property for a new mixed-use development. By analyzing proximity to transportation hubs, schools, hospitals, shopping centers, parks, and other amenities, they can assess the property's desirability and potential for attracting tenants or buyers. Properties located in well-connected areas with easy access to amenities often command higher prices and experience faster appreciation.

Market trends and historical data are also integral to location intelligence. Imagine an agent analyzing historical sales data and price trends in a neighborhood over the past few years. This analysis can reveal patterns such as seasonal fluctuations, long-term appreciation trends, and areas of high demand. Armed with this information, investors can make informed decisions on when and where to buy or sell properties for optimal returns.

In the realm of commercial real estate, location intelligence is especially critical. Imagine a retail developer scouting locations for a new shopping center. By using geospatial analysis, they can identify trade areas, analyze consumer behavior, and understand competition in the area. This deep understanding of the market allows developers to select locations with high foot traffic, strong consumer demand, and limited competition, maximizing the potential for success.

Location intelligence is not just about analyzing static data—it's about dynamic insights that evolve with the market. Imagine utilizing geospatial mapping to visualize real-time data such as foot traffic patterns, crime rates, and property vacancies. These real-time insights allow investors and developers to adapt their strategies in response to changing market conditions, ensuring they stay ahead of the curve.

One of the most compelling aspects of location intelligence is its ability to mitigate risks in property investments. Imagine an investor assessing a property's exposure to natural hazards such as flooding or wildfire risk. Using geospatial data, they can identify properties in high-risk areas and make informed decisions about insurance, mitigation measures, or whether to invest in less risky locations.

Location intelligence is the key to strategic property investments in real estate because it provides a holistic view of a property's surroundings and market context. By leveraging spatial data and analytics, investors can:

- Identify target demographics and tailor properties to meet their needs.

- Assess the economic health and growth potential of an area.

- Evaluate proximity to infrastructure and amenities for convenience and desirability.

- Analyze market trends and historical data to make informed timing and pricing decisions.

- Optimize commercial real estate developments by understanding trade areas and competition.

- Adapt strategies in real-time with dynamic geospatial insights.

- Mitigate risks by assessing exposure to natural hazards and other factors.

In a competitive and dynamic real estate market, location intelligence empowers stakeholders to make strategic decisions that maximize returns and minimize risks. As we navigate the world of data-driven real estate, the importance of location intelligence becomes increasingly clear—it's not just about where a property is located, but about understanding the full context of its location for successful investments.

# Customer Segmentation: Tailoring Deals for Maximum Impact

In the world of real estate, where properties vary widely in size, style, location, and amenities, the concept of customer segmentation is a powerful strategy for tailoring deals to different market segments. Imagine a scenario where one-size-fits-all approaches are replaced with targeted marketing, pricing, and property features that cater to the specific needs and preferences of different buyer groups. This is the essence of customer segmentation in real estate—a strategy that allows professionals to maximize the impact of their deals by understanding and appealing to diverse buyer profiles.

At its core, customer segmentation is about dividing a market into distinct groups based on characteristics such as demographics, behavior, preferences, and buying patterns. In the context of real estate, this segmentation enables professionals to identify and target specific buyer segments with tailored offerings, resulting in more effective marketing campaigns, higher conversion rates, and ultimately, greater success in closing deals.

Imagine an agent working with clients who have different preferences and priorities. By segmenting clients based on factors such as age, income, lifestyle, and family size, the agent can create targeted marketing materials that speak directly to each group's needs. For example, a young couple may be interested in trendy urban condos with proximity to nightlife and dining, while a family with children may prioritize school districts and parks. By understanding these segments, the agent can present properties and neighborhoods that align with each group's desires.

Customer segmentation also plays a crucial role in pricing strategies. Imagine a developer with a range of properties, from luxury penthouses to starter homes. By segmenting potential buyers into groups such as luxury seekers, budget-conscious buyers, and investors, the developer can set prices that appeal to each segment's willingness to pay. This targeted pricing approach not only maximizes profitability but also attracts the right buyers to each type of property.

Moreover, customer segmentation allows real estate professionals to customize property features and amenities to suit different buyer segments. Imagine a developer designing a new residential community. By understanding the preferences of various segments, such as families, empty nesters, and young professionals, the developer can create amenities that cater to each group. This might include playgrounds and schools for families, fitness centers and social spaces for young professionals, and quiet areas for empty nesters. Tailoring properties in this way increases their appeal and marketability to specific buyer segments.

In the realm of commercial real estate, customer segmentation is equally valuable. Imagine a commercial broker working with retail tenants. By segmenting potential tenants into categories such as fashion retailers, restaurants, and electronics stores, the broker can identify properties that align with each tenant's target market. This targeted approach not only helps in filling vacancies faster but also ensures that the property attracts tenants that complement each other, creating a vibrant and successful retail environment.

Customer segmentation also extends to property investors. Imagine an investment firm analyzing potential properties for their portfolio. By segmenting investors based on risk tolerance, investment goals, and preferred asset types, the firm can recommend properties that align with each investor's objectives. For example, risk-averse investors may prefer stable, income-generating properties, while growth-oriented investors may seek properties in emerging markets with high appreciation potential.

One of the most compelling aspects of customer segmentation is its ability to foster long-term relationships with clients. Imagine an agent who not only helps a client find their dream home but also stays in touch with personalized market updates, property recommendations, and investment opportunities. By understanding the client's preferences and needs over time, the agent can continue to provide value and become their trusted advisor for future real estate transactions.

Customer segmentation is a powerful strategy in real estate because it allows professionals to:

• Identify and understand diverse buyer segments based on demographics, behavior, and preferences.

- Tailor marketing campaigns to specific buyer groups, increasing effectiveness and conversion rates.

- Customize pricing strategies to appeal to each segment's willingness to pay.

- Design properties and amenities that cater to the needs and desires of different buyer segments.

- Create vibrant and successful commercial environments by attracting complementary tenants.

- Recommend properties to investors that align with their risk tolerance and investment goals.

- Foster long-term relationships with clients by providing personalized and valuable services.

In a competitive real estate market, customer segmentation is not just a strategy—it's a necessity for maximizing the impact of deals and achieving success. As we navigate the world of real estate, the ability to understand and cater to diverse buyer segments becomes increasingly crucial for professionals seeking to stand out and thrive.

## Transactional Data Management

In the intricate world of real estate transactions, where deals can span from property listings to closings, the effective management of transactional data is crucial for optimizing deal cycles. Imagine a scenario where every step, from listing a property to finalizing the sale, is seamlessly orchestrated with precision and efficiency. This is where transactional data management comes into play, serving as the backbone that streamlines processes, reduces errors, and accelerates the pace of deals.

At its core, transactional data management involves the collection, organization, and analysis of data related to real estate transactions. This data encompasses a wide range of information, including property details, buyer and seller information, financial records, contracts, and legal documents. By effectively managing this data, real estate professionals can streamline workflows, improve decision-making, and ultimately optimize the entire deal cycle.

One of the primary benefits of transactional data management is its ability to centralize and organize information. Imagine an agent with multiple listings, each with its own set of documents, contracts, and client information. By utilizing a centralized database or software system, the agent can access all relevant data in one place, eliminating the need to sift through stacks of paperwork or dig through emails. This centralized approach not only saves time but also reduces the risk of errors and oversights.

Moreover, transactional data management enables professionals to track the progress of deals in real-time. Imagine a broker overseeing multiple transactions. With a transaction management system, they can easily monitor the status of each deal, from initial offer to closing. This visibility allows for proactive intervention when issues arise, ensuring that deals stay on track and deadlines are met. Alerts and notifications can also be set up to keep all parties informed of key milestones and upcoming tasks.

Efficient data management also enhances collaboration among stakeholders involved in a transaction. Imagine a real estate team working on a complex commercial deal. With a shared platform for transactional data, team members can collaborate in real-time, accessing the same documents and information from anywhere. This collaborative approach improves communication, reduces delays, and fosters a more cohesive and efficient team effort.

Transactional data management is also instrumental in compliance and risk management. Imagine a brokerage navigating regulatory requirements for transactions. A robust data management system can store compliance documents, track deadlines for disclosures, and ensure that all necessary paperwork is in order. This not only reduces the risk of legal issues but also provides a clear audit trail for regulatory purposes.

One of the most significant advantages of transactional data management is its role in analytics and reporting. Imagine a brokerage analyzing past transactions to identify trends, such as average days on market, sale-to-list price ratios, and neighborhood appreciation rates. By mining transactional data, brokers can gain valuable insights into market trends, buyer behavior, and pricing strategies. These insights inform future decision-making, allowing professionals to adjust their strategies for optimal results.

For property managers, transactional data management is essential for overseeing lease agreements, rental payments, and maintenance requests. Imagine a property manager using a digital platform to track lease expirations, automate rent collection, and manage maintenance schedules. This streamlined approach improves tenant satisfaction, reduces administrative burdens, and ensures that properties are well-maintained and profitable.

In the realm of investment analysis, transactional data management enables investors to track the performance of their portfolios. Imagine an investor analyzing rental income, expenses, and vacancy rates across multiple properties. With a comprehensive data management system, they can generate reports that provide a holistic view of their investments, identify underperforming properties, and make informed decisions on portfolio adjustments.

Transactional data management is the key to optimizing deal cycles in real estate because it:

- Centralizes and organizes data for easy access and reduced errors.

- Provides real-time visibility into the progress of transactions.

- Enhances collaboration among stakeholders for more efficient teamwork.

- Ensures compliance with regulatory requirements and reduces legal risks.

- Enables analytics and reporting for valuable insights into market trends.

- Streamlines property management tasks such as lease agreements and maintenance.

- Facilitates investment analysis for portfolio optimization.

In a fast-paced and complex real estate market, effective transactional data management is not just a convenience—it's a strategic advantage. As we navigate the world of real estate transactions, the ability to harness data effectively becomes increasingly crucial for professionals seeking to optimize deal cycles, improve efficiency, and achieve success.

# Competitive Analysis

In the dynamic and competitive landscape of real estate, staying ahead of the curve requires more than just intuition—it requires a comprehensive understanding of the market and competitors. This is where competitive analysis, fueled by data-driven comparisons, becomes a strategic tool for professionals to gain insights, identify opportunities, and make informed decisions. Imagine a scenario where real estate agents, developers, and investors have a clear view of their competitors' strengths and weaknesses, allowing them to refine their strategies and stay ahead in the market.

At its core, competitive analysis in real estate involves evaluating and comparing key metrics and performance indicators of competitors in the market. This data-driven approach enables professionals to identify market trends, benchmark their performance, and uncover areas for improvement or differentiation.

Imagine an agent preparing to list a property in a competitive neighborhood. By conducting a competitive analysis, they can compare similar properties recently sold or listed by other agents. This comparison may include metrics such as listing prices, days on market, property features, and final sale prices. This data allows the agent to set a competitive listing price, highlight unique selling points, and tailor marketing strategies to stand out in the market.

Moreover, competitive analysis enables professionals to gain a deeper understanding of market trends and shifts. Imagine a developer evaluating a new project in a neighborhood with several ongoing developments. By analyzing the types of properties, amenities, and pricing strategies of competitors, the developer can assess market saturation, demand trends, and potential buyer preferences. This insight guides decisions on property design, pricing, and marketing strategies to ensure the new project's success.

One of the most valuable aspects of competitive analysis is its role in benchmarking performance. Imagine an investment firm managing a portfolio of rental properties. By comparing metrics such as rental income, vacancy rates, and tenant satisfaction with competitors in the same market, the firm can identify areas where they excel and areas for improvement. This benchmarking allows for data-driven decisions on rent adjustments, property upgrades, and tenant retention strategies to maximize returns.

Competitive analysis is also crucial for commercial real estate professionals. Imagine a commercial broker analyzing office space leasing trends in a downtown area. By comparing rental rates, occupancy rates, and amenities of competing buildings, the broker can advise clients on setting competitive lease terms and attracting tenants. This data-driven approach ensures that clients' properties remain attractive and competitive in the market.

Moreover, competitive analysis extends beyond property-specific metrics to include broader market factors. Imagine an agent analyzing market share data to identify dominant players in a particular neighborhood or property type. This information helps in understanding market dynamics, identifying emerging trends, and adapting strategies to capitalize on opportunities.

In the realm of marketing, competitive analysis is invaluable for crafting effective campaigns. Imagine a brokerage preparing to launch a new marketing campaign for luxury properties. By analyzing the marketing strategies, branding, and online presence of competitors targeting the same market segment, the brokerage can develop a campaign that highlights unique value propositions and resonates with the target audience.

Another key aspect of competitive analysis is assessing the digital presence of competitors. Imagine an agent evaluating online listings and social media engagement of competing agents or brokerages. This analysis provides insights into effective online marketing strategies, popular property features, and customer engagement tactics. Armed with this knowledge, the agent can optimize their own online presence to attract more clients and listings.

Competitive analysis in real estate is essential for staying ahead in the market because it:

• Provides insights into market trends, competitor strategies, and buyer preferences.

• Guides pricing strategies, marketing campaigns, and property design decisions.

- Helps benchmark performance against competitors for continuous improvement.

- Identifies market saturation, emerging trends, and areas for differentiation.

- Guides investment decisions and portfolio management for optimal returns.

- Enhances marketing effectiveness by understanding competitor tactics.

- Optimizes online presence and customer engagement strategies.

In a competitive real estate market, the ability to leverage competitive analysis and data-driven comparisons is a strategic advantage. As we navigate the world of real estate, the insights gained from competitive analysis enable professionals to make informed decisions, refine strategies, and ultimately, stay ahead of the competition.

## Marketing Strategies for Data-Driven Deals

In the fast-paced world of real estate, effective marketing is the key to attracting the right buyers and closing deals. However, in an era driven by data, traditional marketing approaches are being augmented and refined by data-driven strategies. Imagine a scenario where real estate professionals leverage data analytics to understand buyer preferences, behavior, and market trends, allowing them to tailor their marketing efforts with precision. This is the essence of marketing strategies for data-driven deals—strategies that ensure resources are allocated efficiently to reach the most relevant audience and maximize the potential for successful transactions.

At its core, marketing strategies for data-driven deals involve the strategic use of data analytics and technology to identify, target, and engage with the right buyers. By analyzing vast datasets, including buyer demographics, online behavior, social media engagement, and property preferences, real estate professionals can develop highly targeted campaigns that resonate with specific audiences.

**Buyer Persona Development:** One of the foundational steps in data-driven marketing is the creation of buyer personas. These personas are detailed profiles representing different segments of the target audience based on demographics, preferences, behaviors, and motivations. Imagine an agent developing personas such as "Young Professionals Seeking Urban Living" or "Empty Nesters Looking for Downsizing Options." These personas serve as guides for crafting personalized marketing messages and strategies that speak directly to the needs and desires of each segment.

**Hyper-Targeted Advertising:** With data-driven marketing, gone are the days of casting a wide net with generic advertising. Instead, real estate professionals can use data analytics to target their advertising with precision. Imagine an agent using geolocation data to target digital ads to individuals in specific neighborhoods or ZIP codes. This hyper-targeted approach ensures that marketing messages reach those who are most likely to be interested in the property, maximizing the return on advertising investment.

**Personalized Content Marketing:** Content marketing plays a significant role in data-driven strategies, where personalized and valuable content is king. Imagine a brokerage creating blog posts, videos, and social media content that address the specific needs and pain points of their buyer personas. This content not only educates and engages potential buyers but also positions the brokerage as a trusted authority in the market. Personalized content can include neighborhood guides, property market trends, home improvement tips, and more.

**Retargeting and Remarketing:** Another powerful strategy in data-driven marketing is retargeting or remarketing. Imagine a scenario where a potential buyer visits a real estate website but leaves without taking action. With retargeting, that visitor may then see targeted ads for the property they viewed as they browse other websites or social media platforms. This reminder can reignite their interest and bring them back into the sales funnel. Remarketing emails can also be sent to those who have shown interest but have not yet made a purchase, providing additional information or incentives to convert.

**Predictive Analytics for Lead Scoring:** Predictive analytics is a game-changer in identifying high-potential leads among the vast pool of prospects. Imagine an agent using predictive models to analyze lead data and assign scores based on factors such as engagement with listings, website visits, and previous interactions.

These lead scores help prioritize follow-up efforts, ensuring that resources are focused on leads with the highest likelihood of conversion.

**Virtual Tours and 3D Visualization:** In the era of data-driven deals, technology such as virtual tours and 3D visualization is a marketing asset. Imagine a buyer exploring a property through a virtual tour that allows them to "walk through" the home from the comfort of their device. This immersive experience not only attracts tech-savvy buyers but also provides a detailed view of the property's features and layout. Real estate professionals can also use 3D visualization to showcase properties in a realistic and engaging way, capturing the attention of potential buyers.

**Social Media Targeting:** Social media platforms are rich sources of data for targeting the right buyers. Imagine an agent using Facebook's ad targeting options to reach users based on their interests, behaviors, and location. Ads can be tailored to specific demographics, such as age, income, interests, and even life events like "recently engaged" or "newlyweds." This precision targeting ensures that the marketing message reaches those who are most likely to be interested in the property.

**Data-Driven Email Campaigns:** Email marketing remains a powerful tool in data-driven strategies. Imagine an agent sending personalized email campaigns to segmented lists based on buyer personas or previous interactions. These emails can include property recommendations, market updates, upcoming open houses, and exclusive offers. By analyzing email engagement metrics, such as open rates and click-through rates, agents can refine their campaigns for maximum impact.

**Leveraging Reviews and Testimonials:** In the world of data-driven deals, social proof is essential. Imagine a brokerage showcasing positive reviews and testimonials from satisfied clients on their website and social media channels. These endorsements build credibility and trust with potential buyers, encouraging them to consider the brokerage for their real estate needs. Real estate professionals can also use client feedback data to continuously improve their services and offerings.

**Analytics and Optimization:** Data-driven marketing is an iterative process that relies on analytics for continuous improvement. Imagine an agent regularly analyzing campaign performance metrics such as conversion rates, engagement rates, and return on investment (ROI). This data provides valuable insights into what strategies are working and where adjustments are needed. By optimizing campaigns based on this data, real estate professionals can refine their approach and achieve better results over time.

Marketing strategies for data-driven deals in real estate are all about precision, personalization, and effectiveness. By leveraging data analytics and technology, professionals can:

- Develop detailed buyer personas for targeted messaging.

- Use hyper-targeted advertising to reach specific audiences.

- Create personalized content that addresses buyer needs.

- Employ retargeting and remarketing to re-engage potential buyers.

- Utilize predictive analytics for lead scoring and prioritization.

- Showcase properties with virtual tours and 3D visualization.

- Target buyers on social media based on interests and behaviors.

- Send data-driven email campaigns to segmented lists.

- Highlight positive reviews and testimonials for social proof.

- Continuously analyze and optimize campaigns for improved results.

In a competitive real estate market, these data-driven marketing strategies are essential for professionals seeking to target the right buyers, increase engagement, and ultimately, achieve successful transactions. As we navigate the world of real estate marketing, the integration of data analytics and technology is not just a trend—it's a strategic imperative for those looking to thrive in a rapidly evolving industry.

# Risk Assessment Models: Minimizing Losses with Data

In the world of real estate investment, where opportunities abound but risks can loom large, the ability to assess and mitigate risks is crucial for success. This is where risk assessment models, powered by data and analytics, play a vital role in helping investors make informed decisions and minimize potential losses. Imagine a scenario where investors have the tools to quantitatively evaluate risks associated with properties, markets, and economic factors, allowing them to allocate resources wisely and safeguard their investments. This is the promise of risk assessment models in real estate—a strategic approach that leverages data to identify, analyze, and mitigate risks effectively.

**Understanding Risk Factors:** Risk assessment models in real estate begin with a thorough understanding of the various factors that can impact the success or failure of an investment. These factors can include market trends, economic indicators, property characteristics, location-specific risks, regulatory changes, and more. By analyzing historical data and market trends, investors can identify the key risk factors relevant to their investment strategy.

**Quantitative Analysis:** One of the primary benefits of risk assessment models is their ability to quantify risks in a systematic and objective manner. Imagine an investor using a model that assigns numerical values to different risk factors, such as vacancy rates, rental income variability, property appreciation rates, and market volatility. These quantitative metrics provide a clear and standardized way to assess risks, allowing investors to compare different investment opportunities and make data-driven decisions.

**Scenario Analysis:** Risk assessment models also enable investors to conduct scenario analysis, where they simulate different market conditions and scenarios to understand potential outcomes. Imagine an investor modeling scenarios such as a recession, interest rate changes, or unexpected market shocks. By running these scenarios through the risk assessment model, investors can assess the impact on their portfolio, cash flow projections, and overall risk exposure. This proactive approach allows investors to prepare for various eventualities and adjust their strategies accordingly.

**Portfolio Diversification:** Diversification is a fundamental principle in risk management, and risk assessment models help investors optimize their portfolios for diversification. Imagine an investor using a model to analyze the correlation between different asset classes, such as residential properties, commercial properties, and stocks. By understanding how these assets behave in different market conditions, investors can build a diversified portfolio that spreads risk across various sectors and reduces overall volatility.

**Market Risk vs. Property-Specific Risk:** Risk assessment models also distinguish between market risk and property-specific risk. Market risk refers to risks that affect the entire real estate market, such as economic downturns or interest rate changes. Property-specific risk, on the other hand, relates to risks specific to individual properties, such as location risks, tenant turnover, or property condition. By analyzing both types of risks, investors can develop strategies to mitigate each type effectively.

**Risk-Adjusted Return Analysis:** In real estate investment, it's not just about maximizing returns—it's about achieving the right balance between risk and return. Risk assessment models help investors perform risk-adjusted return analysis, where they evaluate the potential return of an investment relative to its level of risk. Imagine an investor using a model to calculate metrics such as the Sharpe ratio or the risk-adjusted cap rate. These metrics provide a clearer picture of whether an investment offers an attractive return considering the associated risks.

**Sensitivity Analysis:** Sensitivity analysis is another valuable tool in risk assessment models, allowing investors to understand how changes in key variables can impact investment outcomes. Imagine an investor analyzing how variations in factors such as rental income, property expenses, or market trends affect cash flow projections and property valuations. This sensitivity analysis helps investors identify the most critical variables and potential sources of risk, allowing for more informed decision-making.

**Due Diligence Enhancement:** Risk assessment models enhance the due diligence process by providing a structured framework for evaluating properties and markets. Imagine an investor using a checklist within the model to systematically assess factors such as property condition, location desirability, tenant profiles, and market trends. This thorough analysis helps investors uncover potential risks and opportunities early in the investment process, leading to better-informed decisions.

**Regulatory Compliance:** In the realm of real estate investment, regulatory compliance is a critical aspect of risk management. Risk assessment models help investors stay compliant with regulations by incorporating factors such as zoning laws, building codes, environmental regulations, and tax implications into their analysis. By considering these regulatory risks upfront, investors can avoid costly penalties and legal issues down the line.

**Continuous Monitoring and Adjustments:** Risk assessment models are not static—they are dynamic tools that require continuous monitoring and adjustments. Imagine an investor regularly updating their risk assessment model with new market data, property performance metrics, and economic indicators. This ongoing analysis allows investors to stay informed of changing market conditions and make timely adjustments to their strategies to mitigate emerging risks.

In summary, risk assessment models in real estate are powerful tools for minimizing losses and maximizing returns by:

• Understanding and quantifying various risk factors.

• Conducting scenario analysis to prepare for different market

# Data Privacy and Security in Real Estate

In an era where data is considered one of the most valuable assets, the protection of sensitive information is paramount, especially in the realm of real estate. From personal client data to financial transactions and property details, real estate professionals handle a vast amount of confidential information that must be safeguarded against cyber threats, breaches, and unauthorized access. This is where robust data privacy and security measures become crucial for maintaining trust, compliance, and the integrity of the real estate industry.

**Importance of Data Privacy:** Data privacy refers to the protection of personal and confidential information from unauthorized access, use, or disclosure. In real estate, sensitive data such as client names, addresses, financial records, credit scores, and property details are collected and stored. Protecting this information is not just a legal obligation but also an ethical responsibility to clients and stakeholders.

**Legal Frameworks and Compliance:** Real estate professionals must adhere to various data protection laws and regulations to ensure compliance and avoid legal repercussions. Imagine an agent handling client data without proper consent or security measures. This could result in violations of laws such as the General Data Protection Regulation (GDPR) in Europe, the California Consumer Privacy Act (CCPA) in the U.S., or industry-specific regulations like the Gramm-Leach-Bliley Act (GLBA) for financial data protection.

**Secure Data Storage and Encryption:** Real estate firms and agents store vast amounts of sensitive data, making secure data storage essential. Imagine a brokerage utilizing encrypted databases and secure cloud storage to protect client information. Encryption ensures that even if data is accessed without authorization, it remains unintelligible and unusable to unauthorized parties.

**Access Controls and Authentication:** Access controls are critical for limiting who can view, modify, or delete sensitive data. Imagine a real estate agency implementing role-based access controls, where employees only have access to the data necessary for their roles. Multi-factor authentication adds an extra layer of security, requiring users to provide multiple forms of verification before accessing sensitive systems or data.

**Employee Training and Awareness:** Human error is a common cause of data breaches, which is why ongoing employee training and awareness programs are essential. Imagine an agency providing regular training on data privacy best practices, phishing awareness, password security, and handling sensitive information. Employees are educated on the risks and protocols for protecting valuable data.

**Secure Communication Channels:** Real estate transactions often involve sensitive communication, such as contract negotiations, financial details, and legal documents. Imagine a broker using encrypted email services or secure messaging platforms to communicate with clients and partners. Secure communication channels ensure that confidential information remains protected during transit.

**Data Minimization and Retention Policies:** Data minimization involves collecting only the necessary data for a specific purpose, reducing the risk of exposure. Imagine a property manager implementing a policy to collect and retain tenant information only as required by law or for legitimate business purposes. Retention policies dictate how long data is stored, ensuring that outdated or unnecessary data is regularly purged to reduce risks.

**Vendor and Third-Party Risk Management:** Real estate professionals often work with vendors, contractors, and third-party service providers who may have access to sensitive data. Imagine an agent conducting due diligence on third-party vendors to ensure they have robust security measures in place. Contracts should include clauses on data protection, confidentiality, and compliance with applicable regulations.

**Data Breach Response Plan:** Despite best efforts, data breaches can still occur. Real estate firms should have a comprehensive data breach response plan in place. Imagine a brokerage having protocols for immediate containment, notification of affected parties, cooperation with authorities, and steps for mitigating further damage. This preparedness can minimize the impact of a breach and protect client trust.

**Transparency and Client Consent:** Lastly, transparency and client consent are essential principles in data privacy. Imagine an agent explaining to clients how their data will be used, stored, and protected. Obtaining explicit consent for data processing builds trust and demonstrates a commitment to respecting client privacy preferences.

Data privacy and security in real estate are critical for:

- Protecting sensitive client and financial information.

- Ensuring compliance with data protection laws and regulations.

- Safeguarding against cyber threats, breaches, and unauthorized access.

- Utilizing secure data storage and encryption measures.

- Implementing access controls and multi-factor authentication.

- Providing ongoing employee training and awareness.

- Using secure communication channels for sensitive transactions.

- Enforcing data minimization and retention policies.

- Managing risks associated with vendors and third-party providers.

- Having a robust data breach response plan and fostering transparency with clients.

By prioritizing data privacy and security, real estate professionals can not only protect valuable information but also uphold trust, integrity, and compliance within the industry. As the digital landscape evolves, these measures become increasingly vital for maintaining a competitive edge while safeguarding clients' confidential data.

## Ethical Use of Data: Ensuring Fairness and Transparency

In an age where data has become a cornerstone of decision-making in real estate, ethical considerations surrounding its use have never been more crucial. Real estate professionals handle vast amounts of data—from client information to market trends—and how this data is collected, analyzed, and utilized can have significant implications for fairness, transparency, and trust. Imagine a scenario where real estate agents, developers, and investors uphold ethical standards, ensuring that data is used responsibly to benefit clients and communities while avoiding harm or discrimination. This is the essence of ethical use of data in real estate—a commitment to fairness, transparency, and responsible stewardship of information.

**Fairness and Non-Discrimination:** Ethical use of data in real estate begins with a commitment to fairness and non-discrimination. Imagine an agent using data analytics to target specific neighborhoods or demographic groups for marketing. While data can provide insights into market trends, it should never be used to discriminate against individuals or groups based on protected characteristics such as race, ethnicity, religion, gender, or familial status. Real estate professionals must ensure that their practices adhere to fair housing laws and promote equal opportunity for all.

**Informed Consent and Transparency:** Central to ethical data use is obtaining informed consent and maintaining transparency with clients regarding how their data will be collected, used, and shared. Imagine an agent clearly explaining to clients the types of data collected, such as personal information, financial records, property preferences, and how this data will be used to facilitate transactions. Clients should have the opportunity to consent to the use of their data and understand the implications before providing it.

**Data Accuracy and Integrity:** Ethical real estate professionals prioritize data accuracy and integrity to prevent misinformation or misrepresentation. Imagine a brokerage ensuring that property listings, market analyses, and client information are accurate and up-to-date. Misleading or inaccurate data can lead to poor decisions and harm both clients and the reputation of the industry. Regularly verifying and validating data sources is essential for maintaining integrity.

**Privacy Protection:** Respecting client privacy is a cornerstone of ethical data use. Real estate professionals must safeguard client information from unauthorized access, breaches, or misuse.

Imagine an agent implementing strict privacy policies, secure data storage, and encryption measures to protect sensitive client data. Clients should feel confident that their personal and financial information is handled with the utmost care and confidentiality.

**Use of Predictive Analytics:** Predictive analytics, while powerful, must be used ethically to avoid bias or discrimination. Imagine an investor using predictive models to analyze rental prices or property values. These models should be trained on diverse and representative data to prevent bias against certain groups. Real estate professionals must also be aware of the limitations and potential biases inherent in predictive algorithms and take steps to mitigate them.

**Responsible Data Sharing and Collaboration:** Real estate professionals often collaborate with other agents, brokers, and service providers, necessitating responsible data sharing practices.

Imagine a brokerage sharing client information with a partner for a joint venture. Ethical considerations require that data sharing agreements are in place, outlining how data will be used, stored, and protected. Clients should be informed of any data sharing arrangements and have the option to opt-out if desired.

**Avoiding Conflict of Interest:** Ethical real estate professionals are vigilant about avoiding conflicts of interest that could compromise their integrity or impartiality. Imagine an agent representing both the buyer and seller in a transaction without proper disclosure. This scenario presents a conflict of interest, as the agent's loyalty may be divided. Transparency about relationships, commissions, and potential conflicts ensures fairness and trust between all parties involved.

**Accountability and Compliance:** Real estate professionals must hold themselves accountable to ethical standards and regulatory requirements.

Imagine an agency implementing internal policies and procedures for ethical data use, with designated individuals responsible for compliance oversight. Regular audits and reviews ensure that data practices align with legal and ethical guidelines, fostering a culture of accountability within the organization.

**Community Impact and Social Responsibility:** Ethical data use extends beyond individual transactions to consider broader community impact and social responsibility. Imagine a developer analyzing data to plan a new residential project. Ethical considerations involve assessing the project's impact on the community, such as affordability, access to amenities, and environmental sustainability. Real estate professionals have a responsibility to consider how their actions and decisions affect the neighborhoods and communities they serve.

**Continuous Education and Ethical Awareness:** Ethical data use requires ongoing education and awareness among real estate professionals. Imagine an industry where agents, brokers, and investors participate in training on data ethics, fair housing laws, and best practices. This continuous learning fosters a culture of ethical decision-making and ensures that professionals stay informed of evolving ethical considerations in a rapidly changing digital landscape.

Ethical use of data in real estate is essential for:

- Upholding fairness and non-discrimination in all practices.

- Obtaining informed consent and maintaining transparency with clients.

- Ensuring data accuracy, integrity, and privacy protection.

- Using predictive analytics responsibly to prevent bias.

- Implementing responsible data sharing practices with agreements and disclosures.

- Avoiding conflicts of interest and maintaining impartiality.

- Holding accountability to ethical standards and regulatory compliance.

- Considering community impact and social responsibility in decision-making.

- Engaging in continuous education and awareness of ethical considerations.

By embracing ethical principles in data use, real estate professionals not only protect clients' interests but also uphold the integrity and trustworthiness of the industry as a whole. As technology continues to advance, the ethical use of data becomes increasingly critical for navigating ethical dilemmas, fostering trust with clients and communities, and shaping a responsible and sustainable future for real estate.

# Regulatory Compliance in a Data-Driven World

In the rapidly evolving landscape of real estate, where data has become a cornerstone of decision-making and business operations, navigating the complex web of legal frameworks and regulations is essential. Real estate professionals handle vast amounts of sensitive information—from client data to market trends—and ensuring compliance with relevant laws is not just a legal obligation but a crucial step towards protecting client interests, maintaining trust, and mitigating legal risks. Imagine a scenario where real estate agents, brokers, and investors are well-versed in the legal frameworks that govern data use, privacy, and transactions, allowing them to navigate the data-driven world with confidence and integrity.

**Data Protection Laws and Regulations:** In the realm of data-driven real estate, data protection laws and regulations are paramount. Imagine a brokerage handling client information, financial records, and property details. Compliance with laws such as the General Data Protection Regulation (GDPR) in Europe, the California Consumer Privacy Act (CCPA) in the U.S., and other regional data protection laws is crucial. These laws govern how personal data is collected, processed, stored, and shared, emphasizing the importance of transparency, consent, and data security.

**Fair Housing Laws and Equal Opportunity:** Fair housing laws are fundamental to the real estate industry, ensuring equal opportunity and prohibiting discrimination based on protected characteristics such as race, ethnicity, religion, gender, familial status, and disability. Imagine an agent using data analytics to target specific demographics for marketing. Compliance with fair housing laws requires that data-driven practices do not result in discriminatory practices. Real estate professionals must be vigilant to avoid unintentional bias in their data analysis and marketing strategies.

**Financial Regulations and Anti-Money Laundering (AML) Laws:** Real estate transactions involve significant financial transactions, making compliance with financial regulations and anti-money laundering laws essential. Imagine an investor purchasing multiple properties with cash transactions. Real estate professionals must adhere to laws such as the Bank Secrecy Act (BSA) and the Financial Crimes Enforcement Network (FinCEN) regulations, which require reporting suspicious activities and implementing due diligence measures to prevent money laundering in real estate transactions.

**Privacy Laws and Consumer Rights:** Privacy laws, particularly those related to consumer rights, play a crucial role in data-driven real estate.

Imagine a broker sending marketing communications to clients. Compliance with laws such as the Telephone Consumer Protection Act (TCPA) and the CAN-SPAM Act ensures that consumers have the right to opt-out of marketing communications and that unsolicited messages are not sent. Real estate professionals must respect consumer privacy preferences and provide mechanisms for opting out of communications.

**Contractual Agreements and Disclosures:** Real estate transactions involve various contractual agreements and disclosures that must comply with legal requirements. Imagine an agent drafting a purchase agreement or disclosure statement for a property. Compliance with state and federal laws, such as disclosure of property defects, lead-based paint hazards, or environmental issues, is crucial. Real estate professionals must ensure that contracts and disclosures are accurate, complete, and compliant with relevant regulations.

**Licensing and Professional Standards:** Real estate professionals are subject to licensing requirements and professional standards set by regulatory bodies. Imagine a broker overseeing a team of agents. Compliance with state licensing laws, continuing education requirements, and ethical standards set by organizations such as the National Association of Realtors (NAR) is essential. Real estate professionals must maintain active licenses, stay informed of regulatory changes, and uphold ethical standards in their practices.

**Data Retention and Destruction Policies:** Real estate firms handle vast amounts of data, and proper data retention and destruction policies are essential for compliance. Imagine a brokerage retaining client records beyond legal requirements. Compliance with data retention laws, such as those outlined in the GLBA for financial data or state-specific recordkeeping requirements, ensures that data is stored for the necessary period and securely destroyed when no longer needed.

**International Transactions and Cross-Border Data Transfers:** In an interconnected world, real estate transactions often involve international parties and cross-border data transfers. Imagine an investor purchasing property in a foreign country. Compliance with international data transfer laws, such as the EU-U.S. Privacy Shield or Standard Contractual Clauses (SCCs), is essential for protecting data when transferred across borders. Real estate professionals must ensure that data transfers comply with the laws of the countries involved.

**Cybersecurity and Data Breach Notification:** Cybersecurity is a critical aspect of regulatory compliance in a data-driven world. Real estate firms are prime targets for cyberattacks due to the sensitive information they handle. Imagine a brokerage experiencing a data breach. Compliance with data breach notification laws, such as those requiring timely notification to affected individuals and authorities, is essential. Real estate professionals must implement robust cybersecurity measures, conduct regular risk assessments, and have a data breach response plan in place.

**Continuous Monitoring and Compliance Oversight:** Regulatory compliance is not a one-time task but an ongoing commitment. Imagine a brokerage regularly reviewing and updating its policies, procedures, and practices to ensure compliance with evolving regulations. Compliance oversight and monitoring mechanisms, such as audits, internal controls, and designated compliance officers, are essential for detecting and addressing potential compliance issues proactively.

Regulatory compliance in a data-driven world is crucial for:

- Adhering to data protection laws and regulations.

- Ensuring compliance with fair housing laws and equal opportunity principles.

- Complying with financial regulations and anti-money laundering laws.

- Respecting privacy laws and consumer rights.

- Creating compliant contractual agreements and disclosures.

- Upholding licensing requirements and professional standards.

- Implementing data retention and destruction policies.

- Complying with international data transfer laws for cross-border transactions.

- Maintaining cybersecurity and data breach notification compliance.

- Conducting continuous monitoring and compliance oversight.

Real estate professionals must navigate these legal frameworks and regulations diligently to protect client interests, maintain trust, and mitigate legal risks in a data-driven world. By prioritizing regulatory compliance, real estate firms and professionals demonstrate their commitment to ethical practices, integrity, and professionalism in an increasingly complex and interconnected industry.

# The Future of Data in Real Estate

As we look ahead to the future of real estate, one thing is certain: data will continue to be a driving force shaping the industry's landscape. The convergence of advanced technology, big data analytics, and innovative applications is revolutionizing how real estate professionals operate, make decisions, and interact with clients. Imagine a future where real-time insights, predictive analytics, and artificial intelligence (AI) capabilities transform every aspect of the real estate lifecycle, from property valuation to marketing strategies. Here are some trends and innovations to watch as the future of data in real estate unfolds:

**Predictive Analytics for Market Forecasting:** Predictive analytics is poised to become even more sophisticated, providing real estate professionals with insights into future market trends and property values. Imagine an investor using predictive models to forecast rental demand in specific neighborhoods or predict future property appreciation. These predictive capabilities empower investors and developers to make data-driven decisions with confidence.

**AI-Powered Property Valuations:** Artificial intelligence is revolutionizing property valuation processes, offering more accurate and efficient methods. Imagine an AI algorithm analyzing vast datasets of comparable properties, market trends, and economic indicators to generate precise property valuations in real-time. These AI-powered valuations save time, reduce human error, and provide more transparency to buyers, sellers, and lenders.

**Virtual and Augmented Reality for Property Showcasing:** Virtual and augmented reality (VR/AR) technologies are transforming the way properties are showcased to clients. Imagine a buyer exploring multiple properties through immersive virtual tours from the comfort of their home. VR/AR technologies offer realistic 3D experiences, allowing clients to visualize layouts, amenities, and design features before scheduling physical visits. This not only enhances the buying experience but also saves time for both clients and agents.

**Blockchain for Secure Transactions and Smart Contracts:** Blockchain technology is gaining traction in real estate for its potential to secure transactions and streamline processes. Imagine a scenario where property transactions are recorded on a blockchain ledger, providing transparent and tamper-proof records of ownership history. Smart contracts, powered by blockchain, automate contract execution, escrow, and payment processes, reducing paperwork and the risk of fraud.

**Internet of Things (IoT) for Smart Buildings:** The Internet of Things (IoT) is revolutionizing property management and tenant experiences. Imagine buildings equipped with IoT sensors that monitor energy usage, occupancy levels, air quality, and maintenance needs in real-time. Property managers can use this data to optimize building operations, reduce costs, and enhance tenant comfort. Tenants benefit from smart features such as keyless entry systems and personalized climate control.

**Data-driven Personalization in Marketing:** Data-driven marketing strategies will continue to evolve, offering personalized experiences for buyers and renters. Imagine a marketing campaign that targets potential buyers based on their specific preferences, such as neighborhood amenities, property size, and style. Real estate professionals can leverage data analytics to create tailored content, advertisements, and offers that resonate with individual preferences, increasing engagement and conversion rates.

**Enhanced Location Intelligence with Geospatial Data:** Location intelligence will be enriched by geospatial data, providing deeper insights into neighborhoods, amenities, and market trends. Imagine an agent using geospatial analysis to identify emerging neighborhoods with high growth potential or areas with high demand for specific property types. Geospatial data enhances decision-making by visualizing patterns, trends, and opportunities based on location.

**Cloud Computing for Scalability and Collaboration:** Cloud computing will continue to be a game-changer for real estate firms, offering scalability, flexibility, and collaboration capabilities. Imagine a brokerage using cloud-based platforms for data storage, analysis, and collaboration among team members. Cloud computing enables real-time access to data from anywhere, enhances data security, and facilitates seamless collaboration on transactions and projects.

**Ethical AI and Bias Mitigation:** As AI algorithms become more prevalent, ensuring ethical AI and mitigating bias will be critical. Imagine an AI model trained on diverse and representative datasets to avoid perpetuating biases in property valuation or marketing. Real estate professionals must prioritize ethical AI practices, including transparency in algorithm decision-making and regular audits to identify and correct biases.

**Data Governance and Compliance Solutions:** With the increasing volume and complexity of data, robust data governance and compliance solutions will be essential. Imagine a brokerage implementing data governance frameworks that ensure data quality, security, and regulatory compliance. These solutions include data management policies, privacy controls, and audit trails to track data usage and ensure adherence to legal requirements.

The future of data in real estate promises a landscape of innovation and transformation, where:

- Predictive analytics forecasts market trends and property values.

- AI-powered valuations revolutionize property appraisal processes.

- VR/AR technologies enhance property showcasing and buying experiences.

- Blockchain secures transactions and automates contract processes.

- IoT optimizes building management and tenant experiences.

- Data-driven marketing offers personalized experiences for buyers and renters.

- Geospatial data enriches location intelligence and decision-making.

- Cloud computing enables scalability, flexibility, and collaboration.

- Ethical AI practices ensure fairness and mitigate biases.

- Data governance and compliance solutions protect data integrity and ensure legal compliance.

Real estate professionals who embrace these trends and innovations will be better equipped to navigate the data-driven future, deliver enhanced services to clients, and stay ahead in a rapidly evolving industry. As technology continues to advance, the possibilities for leveraging data in real estate are limitless, promising a future where informed decisions, efficiency, and client satisfaction are at the forefront of every transaction.

# *Conclusion*

In the ever-evolving world of real estate, the power of data has emerged as a transformative force, reshaping the way professionals operate, make decisions, and create value. As we journey through the chapters of "Data-Driven Deals: Leveraging Technology for Real Estate Success," we have explored the myriad ways in which data is revolutionizing every aspect of the industry—from market analysis to property valuations, customer segmentation to risk assessment.

The future of real estate belongs to those who dare to embrace the data revolution, harnessing its potential to drive innovation, efficiency, and growth. We stand at the precipice of a new era, where predictive analytics illuminate the path to profitable deals, artificial intelligence enhances deal efficiency, and machine learning automates property valuations.

As we envision this future, we see virtual and augmented reality transforming property showcasing, blockchain securing transactions with unprecedented transparency, and the Internet of Things creating smart buildings that enhance tenant experiences and operational efficiency.

Yet, amidst these exciting advancements, we must not forget the ethical imperative that guides our use of data. We are reminded of the importance of fairness, transparency, and responsible stewardship of information. Real estate professionals must navigate complex legal frameworks, uphold consumer rights, and mitigate biases in AI algorithms to ensure a future where data-driven decisions are not just profitable but also ethical.

In the concluding pages of this book, we find ourselves at the intersection of innovation and responsibility. The future of real estate is bright for those who embrace data-driven strategies, yet it is also a call to action—a call to uphold the highest standards of integrity, to protect client interests, and to contribute positively to the communities we serve.

As we close this chapter, let us embark on this journey together, armed with the knowledge, tools, and ethical compass to navigate the data-driven world of real estate. Let us seize the opportunities that data presents, while never losing sight of our commitment to fairness, transparency, and excellence.

The future of real estate is data-driven, and the possibilities are limitless for those bold enough to embrace its potential. The time is now to harness the power of data for real estate success.

Thank you for joining us on this exploration of "Data-Driven Deals: Leveraging Technology for Real Estate Success." May it serve as a guide and inspiration as we navigate the exciting frontier of data-driven real estate.

Here's to a future where every deal is driven by insight, every decision is powered by data, and every success is built on a foundation of integrity.

The future is here. Let's make it ours.

Sincerely, Nella Byran

www.ingramcontent.com/pod-product-compliance
Lightning Source LLC
Chambersburg PA
CBHW050108230526
45470CB00004B/1735